The Book of Hours

Also by Marianne Boruch

POETRY

Grace, Fallen from
Poems: New and Selected
A Stick that Breaks and Breaks
Moss Burning
Descendant
View from the Gazebo
Ghost and Oar (chapbook)

PROSE ON POETRY

In the Blue Pharmacy
Poetry's Old Air

MEMOIR

The Glimpse Traveler

MARIANNE BORUCH

The Book *of* Hours

Copper Canyon Press
Port Townsend, Washington

Cover art: Larry Thomas, *October Drawing, 2010.*
Engraving, acrylic, wax. 22˝ × 15˝.

Copper Canyon Press is in residence at Fort Worden State
Park in Port Townsend, Washington, under the auspices
of Centrum. Centrum is a gathering place for artists and
creative thinkers from around the world, students of all
ages and backgrounds, and audiences seeking extraordi-
nary cultural enrichment.

LIBRARY OF CONGRESS
CATALOGING-IN-PUBLICATION DATA
Boruch, Marianne
The book of hours / Marianne Boruch.
    p. cm.
ISBN 978-1-55659-385-7 (alk. paper)
I. Title.
PS3552.O75645B66   2011
811'.54—dc22

                                        2011010987

98765432 FIRST PRINTING

Copper Canyon Press

Post Office Box 271
Port Townsend, Washington 98368

www.coppercanyonpress.org

ACKNOWLEDGMENTS

Many thanks to the editors of the following journals who first trusted these poems, some in slightly different form: *ABZ, Columbia Poetry Review, Crazyhorse, Denver Quarterly, Field, Great River Review, The Iowa Review, Meridian, Michigan Quarterly Review, Narrative, New England Review, The Normal School, Pank, The Paris Review, Ploughshares, Poetry, Poetry London, Quarterly West, Rattle, Southern Indiana Review, Spirituality and Health, Third Coast, The Yale Review.*

The following poems were included in *Ghost and Oar,* a chapbook published by Red Dragonfly Press, 2007, at the Anderson Center, Red Wing, MN. Grateful acknowledgment to Scott King, founder and editor of that remarkable press.

"My heart, its breathing hole"

"The loon with two chicks"

"Let's review the fog suit"

"Like the silkworm, is it"

"They've made the old fishery"

"Past sixty and pounds over, she"

"Nothing doing, none of it painted, she said"

"Not gracious but hair the wren"

"They collect skulls and go by boat"

"The lake, clouds patch it dark"

Certain places and institutions generously aided and abetted the writing of these poems: residencies from Hall Farm (Townshend, VT), The Anderson Center (Red Wing, MN), the MacDowell Colony, and Isle Royale National Park where I served as Artist-in-Residence; fellowships from the Guggenheim Foundation and the Center for Artistic Endeavors in the College of Liberal Arts at Purdue University. To Brigit Kelly, Joy Manesiotis, and Charles Baxter—my deep and continuing thanks. To Christopher Beach and the students in the theater department at the University of Redlands who staged a black box production of some of these pieces: I'm grateful. Most of all, thanks to David Dunlap and Will Dunlap, as usual my treasured first readers and listeners.

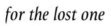

for the lost one

As a tiny seed you sleep in what is small
and in the vast....

—Rainer Maria Rilke, from *The Book of Hours,* 1905

Contents

1 2 **3** 4 5 6 7 8

1 2 3 **4** 5 6 7 8

1 2 3 4 **5** 6 7 8

1234567**8**

The Book of Hours

One may read it walking: lauds and matins

One may read it walking: lauds and matins
and vespers, the major hours. And those minor, at rest,
the little hours in prime and terce, sext and none
and compline, though compline—before bed, blessed

mimic of almost death—*considered separately
by the rubrics.* Their pace, the natural day, dawn
to what follows. The little chapters, canticles, psalms.
Vestments white or red, depending, and violet

for high vigil, black made from the oak gall, once
shrouded by the brilliant toothed leaves.
No antiphon to be repeated the same hour, never
the same words. Advent or Lent or Passiontide,

but *the liturgy of Tuesdays is of no great
character,* not *to purpose or saint or mystery.* Believe
nothing. Or begin: Tuesday, *a day of conflict* like
any, all workweek. Rubrics end best with a semicolon.

1 2 3 4 5 6 7 8

I thought the tree

I thought the tree
beauty. A song, a story. Of
riverbank and good thieves
who took things back and back.

Inside, dampness is dream
of rot and wealth, a holding up,
out, a getting past, a go between
earth and heaven taken down

a notch, to dirt and sky. A bird—
herons favor it high. That's error too.
Eggs fall through, so much light
that weave. Tiny throats raised

in hunger, prickly murmur unto
murmur. Huge eyes in little fists
are blind. It's her heat
dark to that dark, flash of feathers.

I don't like this coolness, she said

I don't like this coolness, she said,
it's not the sound. She liked words
wet or dark, to stop her. But then
she stopped. So hold back,

the voice said. The trick's to
shrink down to *vanish*—not a verb—
where it all looms up. Forget's not
the same as forgive. Those thorny bits

outlast us. Besides, rain was yesterday.
Today light is good, grass
and leaves weigh nothing again.
But the wind, she said. The wind?—

it turns no pages now, hides no fury.
What a *philosophe* you are, she said.
And the voice: See? the poem's
sweet, I'm not duplicitous.

Three kinds of sudden equal three

Three kinds of sudden equal three
windows in a second-story room.
And birds oblivious out there, the way
we borrow something and forget

the kindness, the loss at the other end.
Birds do not suffer. I say that so lightly.
How can you think such a thing?
every mother cries out to me, mother

cloud, mother sideways and thunder,
mother cut with a knife not swiftly,
not clean. Day of almost rain, almost
whoever it was, which of us,

as children. Hidden. Pressed forward
and back. Remote, the urgent
start of it as a door locking distant,
the hinge shuddering up here.

At the laundromat, his close-cropped hair

At the laundromat, his close-cropped hair.
On leave, he bends to the work, cheerful
with strangers. Rolls his socks, creases just
right those jeans. He's not reserve—active

duty army. The real thing, he tells us. Iraq.
Been there. Got the T-shirt, got the fairly
decent pepperoni (really hot dog) pizza
in the Green Zone. And now. What else

does he know—what exploded or did not,
such heat, veiled figures blurring a child
exact, come apart, a wall, a look. He has
perfect posture and socks that drift

like winter on the table. And a room
for those things that lie down
to dream alone. Go nightmare yourself,
he says to them. I can't stop you.

To live in the bird guide, the yellowthroat's

To live in the bird guide, the yellowthroat's
down *thicket* and *hedgerow,* like any
storybook would have it. And maybe his
witchety witchety witchety is *love my life!*

times three. It could be steely: *how dare you*
and *what do you know of migration*
and ice. It's the *edge,* prime happenstance
between woods and field, most ordinary

tangle of vine into brush. But his new
pause before each overdrive triplet
means some weather's coming, *weather*
said secret, with a spike through it.

No. I'm bad weather closing in,
his silence tripped by my noise, my shade.
Four seconds of threat. He's at it again,
his fate to say nothing he says.

The poem puts on its hair shirt, four lines

The poem puts on its hair shirt, four lines
to a stanza. Like a hymn works or a barroom ballad,
a thing that shouts *poem* to any old anyone
walking by. *The lowest common denominator.*

It says that in a book, said the voice to itself,
which would be, for real, what number? two, three?
(Math, as if that needle's eye ever closed.)
At the very least, order, some shade in a quatrain,

a fair amount of daylight—the voice on a roll now—
earth *as is,* circling sun until there's an orbit.
Thinking *pools,* doesn't it? I heard that too.
But how much, how deep? The voice

voiceless, maybe years and years.
Oh scissors cutting paper, rock thrown hard
to break glass. What happens to a thought
come in quiet? Little vast rooms of undoing.

I lost my pen, I lost my keys

I lost my pen, I lost my keys,
and my hat somewhere on a table,
the table its room, the field
its horizon, a road like

a dowsing rod bowed low
to remember, emphatic and forked
that stick, two hands to hold
the map that loved the place, spoke it

day or night I lost in a cellar to dark
and dank where sun tried
for one window—very small—and lost,
over a sink whose water never knew

or kept losing the simplest reason
for coming and going, no way
from the blue or the deep
to bring back a cup of it but a flood.

My mother's body to wires, to tubes

My mother's body to wires, to tubes
and their liquid, days she turned toward me
or away, winter but so much sun
from car to door. I followed it past nurses

at their station talking movies, who's good
in one and not the other. Gown tied
at the back and neck, she slept beside
a window. I wedged my chair there, reading,

looking up, reading—who knows what
I read—her legs bruised, thin, arms battered
by the doctor's needle. Her face. Can I
say this plainly now? There was light

as she grew less. She drifted to it.
I'm not hungry, not religious, I'm in a spot,
she told me one afternoon then
closed her eyes to that radiance again.

1 **2** 3 4 5 6 7 8

Stopped behind a school bus, I saw

Stopped behind a school bus, I saw
the smaller ones run, skip,
burst from the idling open door.
And the larger girl, already so

burdened, pitched forward, the great
sigh of her I could read like words
in any language for *enough,*
for *everlasting,* for *colors that*

darken quickly. The large girl followed
her jubilant sister as if pulled by
a rope woven thick, too many strands.
Early fall, no leaves turning yet,

a little smoke. How the girl moved
behind her sister. Loneliness.
You count backwards for it. So many
things to do. And to become, so little.

I don't know, he said, I guess it's

I don't know, he said, I guess it's
something I'd like, an ocean with such
ugly fish down there dark, ones
with barbs and lantern lights affixed

to their heads. It's all I got, said the voice.
And this wet suit to go with it, this
backpack of oxygen, this camera,
this knife. Be careful. The poem's tough

but one minute it goes delicate on you,
it could dissolve. I don't know, he said,
one leg pushing in, already one arm.
Like his old First Communion suit, white,

even the carnation, the heat that spring,
wilted smell of lilacs. Be almost hypnotized,
the voice said. Remember, punch holes
at the surface. A little breath. What a box.

The usual tacky mosaics one finds

The usual tacky mosaics one finds
in certain hospitals, Christ with a crook
and the sheep, straight up, no
foreground, no background, the colors

off, most of them ghastly. I'd visit
the used-book cart, Harlequin romances
were big. Or the waiting room for surgery
where a guy who wore earphones,

always falling asleep. Outside, men
rose in some high contraption, taken up
to fix whatever needed fixing on the building,
the hospital aware of itself as important,

as *paving the way.* It's not like I knew
the right thing or the wrong thing. Ma,
here comes another one, I'd call out to her,
spooning in the beef puree, the applesauce.

I'll give you a body that won't die

I'll give you a body that won't die,
god whispered in an ear, 643 AD, some
year like that. In a cave or a hut nowhere—
comma—middle of. And isn't that deep down

anyplace? said god. *A body that wouldn't or*
couldn't. I mean, said god, you'll die of course.
But no dust to dust, never to rot. The saint
turned such a thought, and turned it: not

a harbor grateful for ships, not standing
on deck as land comes into sight. Every gift
is a curse, god shrugged. Or the reverse.
They'll keep digging you up. Amazement

like a stain will spread. We walked by
on the trail, figuring sparrow or finch—what is
that trilling? There'll be a cult, said god.
Earth will heave up reason.

He was touched or he touched or

He was touched or he touched or
she did and was, or they were
and would. Or the room could, its
three doors, two windows or

the house on a slant touching,
touched by the drift down street, cars
pressing quick or slowing. All along
the town touched a river, the river

the filth falling through it. What was clean—
a source pure as rumor—a shore
touching lake touched by wind above,
and below, a spring. All touch blindly

further water. That blue touching
blacker regions in the sea so weirdly
solitary, each to under, to every
sideways past deeper, where nowhere.

To make a life inside, you

To make a life inside a life, you
do that—how? My grandmother willed
her chair into a city-state, the porch
a fiefdom, the house itself

a realm. There is music like this,
relentlessly inward. Water meets water
and divides and grows dark all
afternoon at the pond. Down there,

bottom-heavy boxes,
jars, a letter torn in half
and first floated until rain
took it, until even the weave

in the paper unraveled. That life
you wanted secret. Do you
make that? Or does it come and you
remember, it was here once.

She stood there unquiet: a road

She stood there unquiet: a road,
a waterway, all that
luscious distance. About poems, look,
those old 3-D glasses, for movies?—

the voice was building a bridge now,
she could see its rusty parts strewn
along the river. Glasses! I mean the cheap
cardboard kind, plastic lenses, blue

and red, they felt silly going on but
guess what? It wasn't just one
big head anymore, talking to himself—
okay, *her*self—up there. (That

was *it?* The bridge all finished?)
I don't quite, she said, ... those glasses?
A whole other-level retrieval device!
Then the voice stopped saying.

On rain-washed paper dried, ink

On rain-washed paper dried, ink
still blurs. But all words
are stains. The paper's rippled
lunar, mountain and crater,

and *seas* on the moon, misnomer
of plains that looked like
water once, no-end-to-it shadows,
fractal to fractal. The telescope's eye

fooled the eye. From there, does
Earth rise and set? Or a thrush,
would it sing its trouble backward?—
the most private tremor first, then

the public part, famously
melodic but fierce, really it's
fierce: stay   the   fuck   away.
I know that lie, *Sea of Tranquillity.*

1 2 **3** 4 5 6 7 8

It includes the butterfly and the rat, the shit

It includes the butterfly and the rat, the shit
drying to chalk, trees
falling at an angle, taking those moist
and buried root-balls with them

into deadly air. But someone will
tell you the butterfly's the happy ending
of every dirge-singing worm, the rat
a river rat come up from a shimmering depth,

the shit passed purely into scat one can read
for a source, the creature that shadowed it one
longish minute. And trees, of course they
wanted to fall. *It was their time* or something

equally sonorous. And wind too knows its
mindless little whirlpool's *not for nothing,* not
nothing—that pitch and rage stopped. How else
does the sparrow's neck break.

Some dreamily smoke cigarettes, some track

Some dreamily smoke cigarettes, some track
toddlers who walk like drunks. Buzzy,
the picnic grounds, noisy, sun-crazed, how
forks and spoons don't exactly lie flat.

A mountain's here, a famous overlook
from which you'd see none of this. Like that
first daguerreotype, its moving carriages
and those who strolled never picked up

in the long exposure, a Paris street emptied
by the camera, only houses and lampposts
gone eternal. Or the one who stopped
for a shoe shine, the one who knelt to the task.

At the picnic—a commotion. A large man
to a younger man. *I don't know you!* he's hugging
and laughing. *I don't know who you are,*
he shouts over and over a stillness so immense.

You've been walking

You've been walking
the woods again, the voice
called out to him. A bird! What's
a bird to the 21st century?

Or trees? Predictable, way
too happy-happy for poems.
But poison, he said, is nightshade.
And owls hunt hard any

sad small ending. What about
the snake, day or night,
wired as an angel?
Borderline, the voice said,

yo! pony express here!—
have you heard that
phones answer themselves now,
with little messages?

I am so pissed, said god, maybe

I am so pissed, said god, maybe
I'll invent happiness. It was a blur at first.
But it got bigger. It sort of hovered,
wanting to land, to land—

On what? god said to whatever wasn't
bright and brought out of nothingness yet.
Oh that nothing at all—so beautiful, it took
god's breath away. Was it breath?—no,

something else. How long before happiness
turned bluish, restless, trying
to cancel itself out. Should I invent time then?
said god. Maybe the problem is this

summer thing. Maybe trees get sick
of their green and their whispering. Happiness,
said god, welcome! But stand over there,
over there, over there....

In a town I didn't know, yes, I'll wait

In a town I didn't know, yes, I'll wait
by the car. I did. And read there. Wrote
nonsense in a notebook. Considered
the inscription on the bench, one

Karl Thielscher, 1917, athlete, leader, loyal
son, proud parent. A war death. Or maybe
his birth year. Cars rushed the street,
blue, green, a shiny red sun-struck some

painful half-second silver. Those
crossing on foot started, lost faith or grew
brave, the queue infinite, car after car,
the town not large, the only way

to get through it. Maddening. But to
empty like that, waiting, you drift
nowhere really, not care much: a life ago,
I had reasons. Like Karl, I kept track.

Not gracious but hair the wren

Not gracious but hair the wren
weaves into nests is still an offering,
the human head a curious instrument
of giving and use up and get back.

Or hair once crisscrossed into plaster
even now stiffens a wall. The old days.
I told you, that island darks any winter
you want, but more—hurry—one

needs it long. I read he died. She grew
weak alone, iced in out there. No story
at all if not for the rabbit snares
she made with her hair. And watched

in snow, each month adrift. Delicate,
and hopeless it must have, must have
as she knotted and wove, each next one
to make it stinging up from the root.

In the hospital parking lot

In the hospital parking lot,
the huge perspiring priest opened
his trunk and gave me
such lemons: enormous, absurd.

Everyone said I was mistaken.
Everyone later, not believing—*you've
got to be kidding*—then, *really,
lemons!* when I held one

closer, the driving scent of it, proof.
You know we all die,
he said from the car, from
the open window, almost

an afterthought. In fact, it was
a cool day for Florida, even
in winter. A little coolish—that's how
my mother would put it.

So big deal, so you find it sort of

So big deal, so you find it sort of
sucks, the voice said. Fine. Go out
to your regular life where they pay you
for doing something. The poem's

okay in that pile of old papers.
You'll see how you'll empty the day,
be back and open the door. Keys,
even useless ones, have a rattle.

Am I sleeping or writing? she said.
What comes when I call—does it matter
like love matters? Is it sleep who writes?
Or words that sleep? Her eyes had closed.

So many things not clear. Because I keep
telling you, the voice said. It's not like
a person at all. Say it comes like a cat.
Then give up on dreaming that cat.

1 2 3 **4** 5 6 7 8

My heart, its breathing hole

My heart, its breathing hole
at my ear. My head
empties and fills
with it. Like I heard

something in that quiet,
heard the fox, then saw
the fox out there, young, too
early from the den. Was he

in danger? I don't know. It was
lake light, not an ocean
though water came and went, grew
large, the fox probably never

sweet but tentative near the rocks,
not quite, not stopping either. Breathe.
I breathe like that. And gave him
fear. And made him vast.

A *storm darkens the room, rain*

A storm darkens the room, rain
its staccato. But wind's
sideways, a second movement,
a third, loud, off-key then barely

as distant thunder is quiet, deafening
some town a county map away
where they're surprised, it's clear, nothing's
happened yet but *summer afternoon,*

a phrase Henry James called most
beautiful in the language. Language
of desire or forgetfulness. Of pain or
grace. Then smaller, it gets smaller.

I see him walking down
some steps. There are trees and ferns
he'll never notice. The room's still dark.
Next door, every light's gone on.

I do the cat thing, really the dog thing

I do the cat thing, really the dog thing,
cocking my head quizzical. I call up grief
that way and quell it, some treachery,
spite. Wonder has a way of watching

its own amoeba divide: *one part will be*
a brain in thousands of years, one part
a thought there. Time to mull, to catch up
to the speed of resentment or rage. A vacancy,

not even a question. It lies there, filling in
sooner or later. Yesterday I lost
the marked trail, outwitting swampy bits
in the woods, taking dry edges until

I stood still. One minute. Two. You bet it
prayer then: oh cat thing, oh dog thing,
oh how-the-hell-to-get-out thing. Curiosity,
here, *here,* gentle ruler of dread.

On days god had nothing to say

On days god had nothing to say,
a dog still howled, children burst brightly to
pixels in the roadside bomb. A woman out
of Walmart got robbed, the young man

polite at first. Days of pre-settlement oaks, all
bulldozed for a Dairy Queen. The sky rippling
black and gray where corn's pure gold
poured into bottles—it stank a high heaven.

Then god's nothing to say to an ocean
blackened with oil. Wings caught in it, even
the albatross exhausted after miles over the sea
because there were chicks, they were hungry.

Oh but a place in the place of things, it's said
god's nothing to say kept saying. Prayers
beamed up *o help me* and *into thy hands* kept
saying it, circling hours before coming down.

Wish and ache, emphatic

Wish and ache, emphatic—
keep happening, this nothing—
so day after day follows
its morning. That such grace required

night, setting the breakfast table
after supper, hemmed in by sink
and icebox with its Dutch girl decals, each
cup my grandfather placed down dark,

bowls sharply at rest, their shallow.
My grandmother doing spoons, forks, the coffee
she measured. I see them stair by
stair then, sleeping the few hours, folded in

on their sides. But every before-that,
this tempting the next day so
of course and in fact by way of
the table, the old two of them.

The mosquito brings you blood, it

The mosquito brings you blood, it
doesn't bleed you. The voice was sure.
What? he said. Like the bullet's all solace
to the wound? That thing *takes* my blood.

She does, with those eggs inside to consider.
Not true, the voice said. I swear on her
needle of light. Think what she gives you
for nothing, a pinpoint, her single thread

splayed on your arm or aloft at your ear.
Poems, he said, they've wacko-ed you right out!
Knock knock! She siphons my blood to hoard it.
Her dark monotony—*now now now now*—

the whole summer's in it, intrusion and blinding
endlessness, each day without time.
What fun to tell you things, the voice said. As if
I'm wrong—look, how she kneels with it.

Leaf multiplies to tree to make

Leaf multiplies to tree to make
shade finally. You forgot what you
love about light is dark—cool,
precise, suddenly original in woods.

But not simple. I know one legend:
a cripple balled up in an alley
as Peter rushed by. Every saint
throws off shadow. This one grazed

those stunted legs and the man
walked. But how far? And where?
To do what now, all the years
to come. Even the great stories stop

at wonder. And after that? Peter,
man or saint, already up the street,
so busy with infinity, oblivious
to this new trouble he's made.

Some world. No start to it but

Some world. No start to it but
daylight, no stop at dusk. I took
a kayak closer, waterweeds, whatever
they're called in a pond, rushes

from a picture-book bible. The frog's
loud loose thumped
a cello once—that's not right—
then a second time.

Until I showed up. I swear. I was nothing
to that depth. Only blackbirds
kept their hoarse usual. A bloody shard
pinned each wing to flight.

He stared on top of my stare. That frog
was a monster. I don't know
how long. Sit still in a boat and you
swallow yourself whole.

1 2 3 4 5 6 7 8

I woke in rain to old war footage

I woke in rain to old war footage,
the thought that all fighting ends in mud,
in exhausted soldiers walking a road
by the hundreds, not rank and file,

barely holding rifle and pack, a few
bandaged, leaning on others or riding
open-air in a truck. Always the same,
either side. And silent. And little

black floaters on the screen say this is film
but it's definitely over. You can't blink it back,
something ruined and raggedy broke free
in the eye to roam as it wishes. And which

war was that? Those films had one sound,
a forever-was-and-will-be hero voice,
the quietest *why* and *such waste* and the joy
of it stopping numbed by that ballast.

Worry, not to worry, comes

Worry, not to worry, comes
in waves. Small birds freeze, go
dappled in shade, in thickened trees
to miss the hawk. He might

stare past them. His call's shrill
and sweet, dive-bombing from some
height. The vireo, the warbler, the wren
can't—no, they can't be a thing

but dumb and deaf
and blind this instant so nothing
in the woodlot moves or casts
a shadow. *The hawk isn't hungry*

hungry hungry o-mother-o, he
isn't isn't isn't. As if their
silent singing consoles
any of them, or convinces.

The suffering of the masters, Chekhov wrote

The suffering of the masters, Chekhov wrote,
affects the entire household, even those
who work in the garden. Which is to say,
I open his book and my eye finds that

like I found a window once, looked out
to a car, a guy bent to an open door
sullenly arranging, rearranging
for a long trip. Chekhov was hot,

she tells me. And we stare into his picture
on the cover: short hair, a new beard gone
slightly ragged, a young man absolute and hesitant.
Equals *hot,* I agree. Equals something—

It's like we know him, I hear myself. Like
he lives around here. Which is to say, they
keep fighting in the story. I open
to another line: Leave me alone, I beg you.

One gets tired, middle of the day

One gets tired, middle of the day—
not hunger, never lack of love, not
the stricken aspen that
keeps its few leaves left

up high, where wind is
worse. One gets tired thinking,
not thinking, both up all night
in a dream of wires spliced wrong,

the house that fell dark into darker.
One gets tired. It's sudden
like that. A dune shack got tired
all around me once. The sea

broken, kept breaking. And sand
etched those windows endless.
Such a little thing, grass bent low
to make circles in sand. More that.

Let's review the fog suit

Let's review the fog suit
for each island, the voice leaked
from somewhere to tell her. See, you
can't know if it descends *to*

or rises *from* water, even the spruce
bleached out. Close or far, it's not
that pretty. Step out of the fog suit
for the poem. Please. Put on

something else. But I love the fog suit,
she said, rocks eaten by it, minnows
and big honkin' trout, shipwrecks
sticking up in the bay blanked out, guys

who thought they were fishing. Hear it?
They've cut the motor in that nothing.
Only two or three words they repeat,
slowly repeat. And not to each other.

Memory must be viral

Memory must be viral,
the flash
and sting. It rises like
a welt, blisters

then breaks, stone
crushed by
something falling. Where
that comes from, you

think sky and a pretty color
but blue is delirious.
Behind it—night
proves this—you see stars

burning centuries ago.
It takes that long,
every troubled
pin of light.

I've had it with poems, he said

I've had it with poems, he said,
all that once, twice, up, down....
Good, the voice sang, soundtrack
to landscape now, to this or

thatscape where smoke comes out
of chimneys like kids draw a house.
So live there! the voice kept singing.
If I were human, my nephew

would draw such a place. Note
the brickwork. The standard red
but crooked enough to charm.
That's just it, he said. I don't

want charm. I want incisors,
molars with hard silver in place of
such rot. Why not gold? the voice,
shiny from that rooftop.

Those visits home, the way the young

Those visits home, the way the young
come back and still follow you around
or find you on the bed reading
or writing, to lie down at an angle or

sit cross-legged. No secret between you,
not even trouble quite though
it isn't ordinary, the way the world unravels
through them: what he said, what she

never, who traveled where, that things—
how exactly—splinter and break
and cut. It trails off then. Both of you,
which one to speak but thinking

better of it. And the book is just a prop,
what you were writing perfectly weightless
in this silence. Child, oh fully no longer,
out there tangling, untangling.

1 2 3 4 5 **6** 7 8

Past sixty and pounds over, she

Past sixty and pounds over, she
jumped from the boat, suddenly bigger
than her life. Perhaps you were her sister
shocked, who turned away. Because

she stripped off everything, descending—
a goddess, no, a god—in that bright
lagoon where shade made deeper pools,
lake a further noise past those islands.

The truth is, massive and pale, she
lengthened and swam, maybe singing out
something. And why not? I see water so
clear in this story, summer, the grace

to do that, the perfect nerve of any afternoon
marked by abandon, years and years
released like a latch: light and leaves,
remember? Too much and so many.

Note the sky, the voice said. Some say

Note the sky, the voice said. Some say
the poem can read it. One line might start
the cloud thing. It's possible *nimbus*
means quick, that *cumulous* layers up

a lifetime of sorrow. But they all black out.
And release their rain. Their pyromaniacs
do lightning down, in a jag, a razorblade.
Stop! she said. I *know* all this. Jeez.

Because it rains, the voice said. It's raining
right now. And somehow that river
takes back those tears. But fish are key,
fish so stupid about it, their dull glittering

where it's shallow and light gets through.
Light? she said, you said *clouding up a storm.*
You said *the world goes dark.* What else
in there I can't see? All this roundabout.

They collect skulls and go by boat

They collect skulls and go by boat,
knowledge an island, after all.
They circle it. You can tell anything
by bone in the head.

Press this, he says. It's thinning.
This moose lived a long time.
And this one, the carcass found
by wolves that might have

starved, snow two feet deep.
When and how—someone marked
exact, in ink. So this village of skulls
has heroes. The cedar's enormous,

throwing its shade. Bone where
brain kept storm and sky. Lake dizzied
in there. That ache, that dotted line
between us? Their holes stare anyway.

Honest-to-god color, god said, for artists

Honest-to-god color, god said, for artists.
But first, graveyards, to grind the human femur
in secret, for bone-black. And cuttlefish
for sepia, ingenious spray when they

fear things, which is mostly in that water.
For blue, miniature wars to come, pilgrimages,
and rapes some will consider a hobby.
The trade routes: mules, slaves bent low with cobalt

or lapis. And yellow? From piss, out of cows eating
only mango leaves. That will be rumor, little dried cakes
of it. What color am I? thought god, just past
the Ice Age. *Let there be mirrors!* though nothing

looked anything like god in them, world
coming to detail quickly, over eons. Leaf. Rattle.
Out of trees an owl frenzied, mobbed by five
shrieking crows. Red is blood-red eventually.

In the crosshairs of mystery, they

In the crosshairs of mystery, they
say to say: *you can let go now* (mother,
father, fill-in-the-blank). *I know you're only
holding on for us.* Imagine. But imagine

the body. Imagine only half scenes and flashes,
decades of nothing between. You're eighty,
in a diaper, everyone too nice, words
fast, too faint, making over the pretty flowers.

How many IVs? How much oxygen?
Our sitting there, our staring—she did let go of that,
the room, the cheap chairs, let go of Mondays, the guy
bringing the host to her from Mass, gravely aware

of his part in the drama, then someone else
entirely when no, she turned away.
Later, how to find her? I tried blurting out.
I tried letting go of the sentence, midsentence.

The computer screen, day or night

The computer screen, day or night,
illuminated as a manuscript those monks
nameless and famous, eked out repeatedly
for safekeeping, paint fully toxic

in the brightest bits. And why not be
frivolous? The Dark Ages. Hordes or rumors
of hordes. Everyone pretty much dead
by forty. I know, their gardens amaze me.

White rose and red, four kinds of lily, rosemary,
grape. And music past plainchant to eerie
and multiple as the veery in dank woods. His
two-throated song sweetly chokes itself, echo

upward as it's back, go back. So the computer's
every word is black letter and takes out a little light.
To put where? save from what? O the monks,
brilliant and meticulous at their poisons.

There once was a shoe and a coat

There once was a shoe and a coat,
a cell phone, a winter night
locked, unlocking the word
for no words,

a click, a hanging up.
There was one moon. Stars.
A walking to,
not far. Once was drink

and dark, a small room
in the brain where no thought
or two thoughts. Once silence pinned
distance by shouts, a car

grinding toward its lurch
in snow. Once dream. Once
once. Or it's carried back and back.
The body. No, it can't.

Like the silkworm. Is it

Like the silkworm. Is it
spit the spider
leaves behind? Loose
tangle of squares

and circles so moth
and fly go stupid
to pass through or rest
on a thread. Not yet,

either one, though wind
billows the doorway.
She does a little repair,
down, sideways.

A hunger so elaborate
is casual now. Nothing
to it but the rising
and the falling.

1 2 3 4 5 6 7 8

It isn't that serious before dawn, trees

It isn't that serious before dawn, trees
not pressed into service
by light yet. Birds are vague.
It's not the way

the violinist's A string
breaks, middle of the cadenza.
Like my brother showed me
a view from the roof—

we didn't jump—then how
our childhood fit the nail he
pounded, for practice. Memory,
he said, take that. That's

a beginning. The first sound in woods
is alarm: *who walks here.* Soon all
quiets and continues. And I'll
be some other thing.

You say you turn off the jet

You say you turn off the jet,
said the voice, and poems keep coming?
Clever boy! I've heard of that. It's
the holy ghost stuck in his pajamas.

I just want to sleep, he said, god-awful
flood. Not even a spoon
to catch it. Anyway, it's nonsense, gibberish,
some gear losing a tooth each orbit.

No mishmosh allowed! cried the voice,
no thingamajigging! And Chaucer
never spelt it right: *soote* and that
perced to the roote.

For once, please..., he said.
And the voice: okay okay. Let's see.
I know you have a big day tomorrow.
And you   love   your   bed.

Life Studies II: this pencil, this paper

Life Studies II: this pencil, this paper.
The young man slips from his robe,
stretches out, awkwardly fixed on the far
window's blue nothing. Helps to be older,

doesn't it? To draw right at him and not
at him, both. The start, the finish, it's all
about the body, just to leave it somewhere.
Who keeps saying that? In fact, she began

with the divan, the tree dragged into the studio
in its planter, only then that leafy shade
to his shoulder. His pale hip. His penis frail
and awry in a cloud of hair—a shock, a moment

lost. No. No, everything's unbelievable.
You got this far. A whisper or it wasn't at all.
Back there, her body that new, the same
dumb animal in her, looking out.

They've made the old fishery

They've made the old fishery
an old fishery again, real
trout in a waterbox
under the floorboard you

lift by an iron ring. Look.
One's huge. And doesn't even
bother to circle as the smaller
ones circle. Their fate

is anyone's fate. Two choices:
you can wait in that depth
or up here. Meanwhile, flowers
riot in their window and roses

come hither, hither, almost
indecent, then truly. This lost
or never at all held
in that fragrance.

Birdsong, face it, some male machine

Birdsong, face it, some male machine
gone addled—repeat, repeat—the damage
keeps doing, the world ending then starting,
the first word the last, etc. It's that

etcetera. How to love. Is a wire
just loose? Build an ear for that. Fewer, they say.
So many fewer, by far. He's showing off
to call her back. Or claiming the tree.

Or a complaint—the food around here,
the ants, the moths, the berries. She's making
the nest, or both are. In feathers, in hair or twigs,
in rootlets and tinfoil. Shiny bits seen

from a distance, a mistake. But fate
has reasons to dress up. Stupid
and dazzling have a place, a place, a place
though never. She can't sing it.

All this water, what to do with it

All this water, what to do with it?
Dye it a good mood, said god. Or gray,
god said, not feeling so hot. But leave
the foamy bits white. Or it's

reversed. On the bright side, god's
bored, so it's lash and wave. We're little
wire toys in that boat. And calm days,
days where it seems *all praise to,*

the very words writ into lyrics—
really it's seething just under that
godlike good taste. I love these
clichés, said god, how you twist

black to white and read it like
a mirror. Idiots. I'll call it *lake.*
And dream you didn't make me up
to have reason. Sure, I made everything.

Those from the garden, orphaned back

Those from the garden, orphaned back
to woods and meadow: wild geranium
or columbine, wild rose
with its sweet snare. And wild

carrot, its one tiny black
inkling off-center, lace made
by a queen where blood left its mark,
I like to think my mother

told me in that hospital
half-light. Out of her distance of
under and over
briefly, talk of time and time again,

the crooked way someone held himself,
this face or that. *I had such fun*
with you guys, she looked up
the long moment into us.

The screech owl's little horse

The screech owl's little horse
right before dawn. It neighs, it falls
at an angle, in broken bits. Who could
dream this? Who could dream past it?

Little horse out there dark, little
wrenched-from-its-feathers as if
to cry like that gets the world to release
its warmth, the trill hits and drops *here,*

I'm here-re-re, pulled apart. The expanse
in this dollop of wilderness between
house and fence, door and alley. To own
the tree's shadow there, to say

the thing precise and stricken
and not of this earth. I'm never little
as you think, says the owl's
little horse. I watch. And I want.

1 2 3 4 5 6 7 8

Nothing doing, none of it painted, she said

Nothing doing, none of it painted, she said.
A house of wood that says
wood, knots in the grain where a branch
had hope afloat in each board,

windows cut into wall. A wall?
the voice said, you mean a thing nailed up,
hammer hitting square or not? And I
want water in the poem, she said, seen

from a porch. Its blue could be closer.
A pond. An inland lake. Smallest color on a stamp
where no roads can be built. And fish fish fish?
the voice throwing its voice sounded funny,

like a mouse, a little bird: *just the thought
of their flashing....* Don't make fun of me,
she said. They come flush with some
larger world. And I'll forget you.

The loon with two chicks

The loon with two chicks.
No. Two loons with two chicks
equals four. Really three,
he told me. One chick

survives. For now, it's daylight
and glare. And water run. To dip
a hand from the boat, a semisweet
stinging. The air's cut

through thousands of spruce
to get here and smell
like this. How to know the woods
is straight violence and sex,

that anything can walk off
a postcard into ruin, that wolves
track an old moose five at a time.
The bloody *at it* comes quick.

Heads-up! the voice double-whammied him

Heads-up! the voice double-whammied him.
Over there, we got cows—albeit their backsides first.
Velvety cows, brown and white and whatnot.
We got semihuman pasture, we got a pond.

Your point is? he shot back.
Nice nice wild, the voice said, nice enough.
But *hereee*! this side of the path
is wild wild, freak-you-out wild. Twisted,

fallen big, these woods. Nothing is but it isn't. Birds
whine like cats. Dogs up there—geese, *their* barking.
Well duh, he said, I told you.
It's worse, the voice said. They give a rat's ass

about you? And what goes on in that river, you don't
want to know. But poems!—oh that voice, on
and on—*poems* want to know. It's noon, shadows
lie straight under trees. Go, slip through.

When's a fork a spoon

When's a fork a spoon
or a spoon a fork, little
tines stinging out at the end?
Weird and not right but

handy, she insisted. And *runcible,*
good, long-lived. The owl,
the pussycat—you know that poem—
out to sea in a beautiful boat

by a small guitar, my love
and the rest of it.... But a spoon
with those straightaway thorns. A fork
flooding up to the brim. Next

they'll razor the edge and call it
knife. What to cut then?
Once a tongue and a mouth.
And anything you gave it.

So they do, they dive in

So they do, they dive in
in lifesaving class, the girl who
can swim saving the one there
first, pretending her stillness in water,

near death unto death, that drift
impossible to know one whit inside out.
Now her arms, a cartoon of giving up
and going under. How much harder,

practicing ineptitude, the last breath.
The one in a rush to be heroic must think
easy, to draw the drowning soul
back to its body, to restore

the ordinary day. Easy. Until—
give her a fight—scared—you're choking!
It's love, isn't it? To practice, oh practice
like the simplest zealot practices doom.

Is this a mantra? mantra of

Is this a mantra? mantra of
dust—I don't know I
don't know I don't know—mantra
of the million times one says

a million times. Our mother floated
between us at the end like some
island adrift, broken off
the continent. And we kept alert

for sightings, stirrings, any
coming to that might
might might—another
mantra we kept at each night,

returning to that house
with her not in it.
But she's not in the hospital either—
my brother, so bluntly.

The lake, clouds patch it dark

The lake, clouds patch it dark.
And below, trout only want it calm,
no eels to sucker them down or
scar them, no hooks tied with feather.

It's not what you want, the voice said.
And what the moose wants?—not
to be riddle-stung by ticks,
blood gluttons swollen half an inch

by late winter. And what the wolf wants—
guess. Those ravens circle his kill,
birds that will and want some
and already have. It's not

the poem you want, the voice
rang in her ear. As if
you even could—the *finally,* the
never finished in all this.

A shadow. And the bird feigns a broken wing

A shadow. And the bird feigns a broken wing,
dragging away from the nest. She makes a sound
never heard before. Fear hot-wired to hope
is sacrifice. You can pretend to be broken, the pretense

still a wound. As for a higher power: of those
chicks in the nest oblivious, beaks bigger
than any part of them, wide open, the great pin
of dark in there. Anthony, saint to recover the left-behind,

the hidden, who came when I *dear Saint Anthony, please*
look around, something is lost that must be found
over and over as we tore apart the house for years looking.
Was it always keys? Or words on a scrap of paper?

I know it's funny. *Works for peace of mind too,*
the nun too fragile for the front of the room
barely, then couldn't say. I'm here to tell you
that other ache: please, nothing find us.

About the Author

Marianne Boruch's six previous poetry collections include *Grace, Fallen from* (Wesleyan, 2008; paperback edition, 2010) and *Poems: New and Selected* (Oberlin, 2004). She has written two books of essays on poetry—*In the Blue Pharmacy* (Trinity, 2005) and *Poetry's Old Air* (Michigan, 1995)—and a memoir, *The Glimpse Traveler* (Indiana, 2011). She teaches in the M.F.A. program at Purdue University, and in the low-residency graduate Program for Writers at Warren Wilson College. Her awards include Guggenheim and NEA fellowships, a residency at the Rockefeller Foundation's Bellagio Center, Pushcart Prizes, and a Fulbright in the United Kingdom.

 Since 1972, Copper Canyon Press has fostered the work of emerging, established, and world-renowned poets for an expanding audience. The Press thrives with the generous patronage of readers, writers, booksellers, librarians, teachers, students, and funders—everyone who shares the belief that poetry is vital to language and living.

MAJOR SUPPORT HAS BEEN PROVIDED BY:

The Paul G. Allen Family Foundation

Amazon.com

Anonymous

Diana and Jay Broze

Beroz Ferrell & The Point, LLC

Golden Lasso, LLC

Gull Industries, Inc.
on behalf of William and Ruth True

Lannan Foundation

Rhoady and Jeanne Marie Lee

National Endowment for the Arts

Cynthia Lovelace Sears and Frank Buxton

Washington State Arts Commission

Charles and Barbara Wright

To learn more about underwriting
Copper Canyon Press titles, please call
360-385-4925 ext. 103

The Chinese character for poetry is made up of two parts: "word" and "temple." It also serves as pressmark for Copper Canyon Press.

This book is set in RemingaPro and Reminga Titling, fonts designed by Xavier Dupré. Book design and compositon by Valerie Brewster, Scribe Typography. Printed on archival-quality paper at McNaughton & Gunn, Inc.